ART LESSONS FROM GRANDMA

having fun, creating love and learning about life

Denise Weiner • Mikayla Houston

Illustrated by Marie T. Martinelli

Additional copies of this book can be purchased at
www.artlessonsfromgrandma.com

Published by Creative Life Press
www.creativelifepress.com

ISBN: 0988437414
ISBN-13: 9780988437418

This book has been given to

artist

on

date

by

who loves you very much

This book is dedicated to all my cheerleaders who have given me the courage to be my true self, especially Mark, who is always there for me, no questions asked.

INTRODUCTION

This is a book about me.

I love to do art and I love my Grandma.

She teaches me many things as we paint together. We also dream together and have fun. I am very lucky that Grandma introduced me to art when I was very young.

Art is my talent and I will continue to do art all the time as I grow up. Maybe one day, my art and Grandma's art will be in a museum together. For now, we'll just have fun, learn about art and love each other.

You'll see some words in red in the book. These are big, important words that Grandma has taught me. If you don't know what they mean, you can look them up in the back of the book.

Mikayla Houston

This is a book about art and life.

It is about learning important life lessons, developing a positive attitude and, most importantly, building a relationship with a child by making art together.

This is a true story, as told by my granddaughter, Mikayla, when she was 8. Interestingly, I learned as many art lessons from her as she did from me.

Mikayla and I have put her story on paper so that the inspiration and aspirations she has discovered through art can be yours as well.

Denise Weiner

CONTENTS

I was too little to feed myself when Grandma began to teach me about art. She covered the tray of my high chair with a big piece of paper and gave me a big brush.

The paints were in a special container so I couldn't spill them. At first, the brush felt funny in my hand, but Grandma said that when magical colors went onto the paper, I started smiling and giggling. I was excited because the feeling was very new. Grandma loved my first painting and hung it up right away on her refrigerator. I felt very proud.

When I was older, I thought it looked like scribble scrabble. But Grandma said famous artists like Cy Twombly painted that way on purpose. Someone even paid over 2 million dollars for one of his paintings called *Leda and the Swan*. His kind of art is called abstraction.

Now I know that Grandma was building my confidence when she said these things. Because she believed in me, I believed in myself.

I hope someone will buy one of my paintings for a lot of money someday.

When I was old enough to feed myself and walk, Grandma took me to an art class. I loved going there and I loved holding her hand when we crossed the street. I loved the big shirts they let us wear. I didn't love getting my hands dirty. The clay was yucky and the finger-paints were messy. But Grandma knew I'd like using the clay and the paint if I tried them.

First, she painted both of my hands with lots of colors. It tickled. Then, she pushed my fingers around the paper. Wow, was that fun!

Next, she took me to the clay table and showed me how I could make snakes and other neat things. I loved how she helped me play with the clay and paints.

When we were finished with the clay and paints, Grandma helped me onto the special stool so I could reach the big sink to wash my hands. Then we had snacks.

Now I know Grandma was inspiring me and encouraging me to try something new. She said that it's OK to feel a little uncomfortable at first and eventually it will feel more natural. The important thing is to try.

LESSON FROM GRANDMA

Happy surprises can happen if I let them.

One day, Grandma sat with me while I glued white feathers, ribbons and white shapes onto a black triangle. Her white coffee spoon fell onto the paper and stuck there. Even though I didn't plan this, I liked the way it looked and I left it there. Then I sprinkled everything with silver glittler. I really liked the way it looked. Grandma called my artwork a collage. She said it felt like a party.

Another time, Grandma folded a piece of paper and told me to put some paint on one half. She said, "Watch this." Then she folded it and opened it up. I didn't know what to expect and neither did she. But something incredible happened—there was a big design. I saw two yellow ghosts and Grandma saw two beautiful pink birds. Grandma explained that it was OK for me to see the picture my own way because we each see things from our own perspective.

Grandma framed this happy surprise and put it where everyone can see it. I feel proud to see my art in Grandma's house.

Grandma had her first art show when she was 50 years old. She made sure I didn't wait that long. I was 2 when the spiral mobile I made was in a show at my art class. My family came to see my mobile hanging on the wall and we all had cookies and juice.

Everyone took pictures of my art so I would always remember this special day.

The next year, Grandma put the black-and-white collage from my art class in her own art show. All her friends said it was wonderful to see it hanging with Grandma's paintings. They thought it looked like a party too.

I'm very lucky that Grandma does art with me all the time. She didn't do art until she was a grown-up, but she says she feels like a kid when we color and paint together. When I see her having so much fun, I know it's OK to have kid fun, even when you're a grown-up. She always encourages me and is a good example for me.

I hope her paintings will be in an art museum one day.

We are never too young or too old to show the world what we can do.

BY
MIKAYLA

LESSON FROM GRANDMA

I have the power to create my own adventures and I can do anything if I try hard.

At nap time, Grandma often read me two of her favorite books with big, positive messages. The first one is *Harold and the Purple Crayon*. In this story, Harold has a magic purple crayon that he uses to create his own adventures. He can create an ocean and a boat to sail on the ocean. He can draw a mountain, climb it and make a balloon to hold onto when he starts falling off the mountain. He is very good at using his imagination to make his dreams come true.

Her other favorite book is *The Little Engine that Could*. The little blue engine helps push a large train up a big mountain when no other train will do it. The other trains think it's too hard and they're too tired. It's hard, but the little engine kept saying, "I think I can, I think I can." And it brought the big train up and over the mountain. All the children were happy to see the train. And the little engine was very proud!

These books make me think I can do and be anything I want when I grow up. I know I want to be an artist. But I would also like to be a princess and a doctor—or maybe a teacher. Grandma is always impressed with what I do. She's a really good cheerleader.

Every time Grandma goes to an art museum, she buys me books about artists so I can learn about them and the way they make their art. I don't always understand the art in the books, but Grandma says I will when I get older. I enjoy looking at the artwork, even Andy Warhol's paintings of big soup cans and paintings where Pablo Picasso puts a nose where the ear should be. Art can be crazy sometimes.

At art class, I discovered that everyone has their own way of making art and expressing themselves. Grandma taught me not to laugh at other kids' pictures and to appreciate their differences, even if I don't understand them. She explained that even though I may not understand someone's ideas, I can respect them, learn from them and become a better person.

Grandma told me she'll take me to big art museums in New York when I get older. There are many great places where I can see all kinds of art and artists' expressions. She also promised that she'll take me on an art vacation to a faraway place when I feel comfortable leaving Mom for a week.

I have a tea set I made with Grandma when I was 3 and then baked in the oven so we could drink from it. There is no other tea set like it in the whole world. It took me a long time to paint it because I added one mark of color at a time. I feel so proud when Grandma and I use it to play teatime.

One day when we were having a tea party, I dropped a cup on the floor and it broke. I cried because I loved it so much. Grandma put her arms around me and kissed me until I stopped crying. Then she told me she could fix it. I really didn't think she could, but she took out the glue and put each piece back together in a loving way. The cup was as good as new. I was so happy.

LESSON FROM GRANDMA

Be careful with fragile things. But remember that broken teacups and broken hearts can be fixed.

Grandma volunteers with an organization that helps children who have problems in their families. The children go to a studio to use dance, music and painting to express their feelings. Grandma says making art can make them smile and help their hearts feel better.

In school, we have lots of rules. At home, there are lots of rules too. I'm learning that with art, there really are no rules. That's what makes it so great!

Artists like Georgia O'Keeffe, Jackson Pollock and Pablo Picasso created new ways to make paintings and express themselves. They didn't worry about old rules or what others would think of their new ways. They always followed their own hearts and imaginations.

LESSON FROM GRANDMA

I don't need to follow any rules when I make art. I can even make my own rules.

Grandma shows me how to use many kinds of art materials, but she lets me use them any way I want. I really like that. When I make pumpkins for Halloween, I paint them with any face I want and add things like hair, earrings, hats or crowns. My pumpkins don't follow the rules. They have their own personalities.

mikayla

Grandma said she loved to have fun and use her imagination when she was a little girl. She would play hopscotch, ice skate, ride carousels and create things with her crayons and clay. But when she grew up, she went to work at an office and became a mom. Then it seemed like there wasn't enough time for fun anymore. She didn't even learn to paint until she was 48 years old! I think this is why she loves when we spend time together—just her and me—making art.

All our projects are fun and Grandma has the chance to do kid stuff again. She giggles a lot and makes me laugh when she does silly things like putting red paint on the tip of her nose when we paint pumpkins.

LESSON FROM GRANDMA

You're never too old or too young to have fun.

She loves Halloween and thinks it's great to dress up. One Halloween, she wore a fancy mask with feathers. She really surprised me! I had no idea who she was. The next year, when I was Cinderella, she dressed up as an artist with a red beret and a painter's palette. Since she really is an artist, I wasn't surprised. I liked how it felt for us to be dressed up and enjoying Halloween together.

I help Grandpa plan all of Grandma's birthday parties to be sure they're filled with fun. Grandpa takes me to buy party hats, balloons and special cakes to go along with the theme. I also make other decorations, a card and sometimes costumes. Some of the party themes we've had are: Hello Kitty, Dora the Explorer and Hannah Montana. After the parties, I usually get to go home with the balloons and decorations so I can have parties with my dolls.

Grandma encourages me to take chances when I draw and paint. Although I try hard to make the picture look like the thing I'm drawing, such as an apple or a tree, it doesn't always turn out the way I want. When I was younger, I cried when that happened. But Grandma showed me tricks to help me see my picture in a different way, even if I don't like it at first. She said I can:

- put a small frame around it and cut off the part I don't like,
- cut it into several pictures,
- make a bunch of bookmarks from the picture and give them away as gifts, or
- stand on my head and look at it upside down.

One day, I was making a painting of a bell for a friend, but it didn't look like a bell when I was finished. I remembered what Grandma said. I didn't cry. I turned it upside down and saw something else—the bottom of an angel's gown and feet. So I added wings, a head and a halo. I loved it. Now I know if I mess up, I can always change it into something else. I don't get upset anymore if my first try looks bad or messy.

LESSON FROM GRANDMA

Sometimes I just need to look at things from a different perspective.

When Grandma and I are together, she teaches me big words like creativity and cooperation. One new word that's a very big idea is collaboration. This is when people work together and combine ideas. Until I learned that word, I didn't know that Grandma and I were collaborating when we did art together. Usually, I have an idea and she has an idea. When we put them together in a creative way, Grandma and I collaborate and we create things that are awesome.

One time, Grandma showed me a painting she made of a palm tree she didn't like. She asked me what we could do to make it more interesting. I found some animal stickers in our art treasure chest and put them around the palm tree. The picture looked much more interesting. Now it wasn't just a painting. It had become a mixed-media collage. Grandma loved it and so did I!

We also created artist aprons together. Grandma wrote our names on them with fabric paint. Then, I decorated them with designs. They turned out great. Someone in Grandma's art class took a picture of her wearing the apron when she painted a portrait of me blowing bubbles. Grandma took a picture of me wearing mine when we painted our pumpkins.

Now that my apron is too small for me, Grandma is going to buy a new one for me and one for my little sister, Maya. I can put our names on them and Maya can do the decorations. Grandma, Maya and I will collaborate as a team. I'm hoping Maya will sit still long enough for all of us to work on them together.

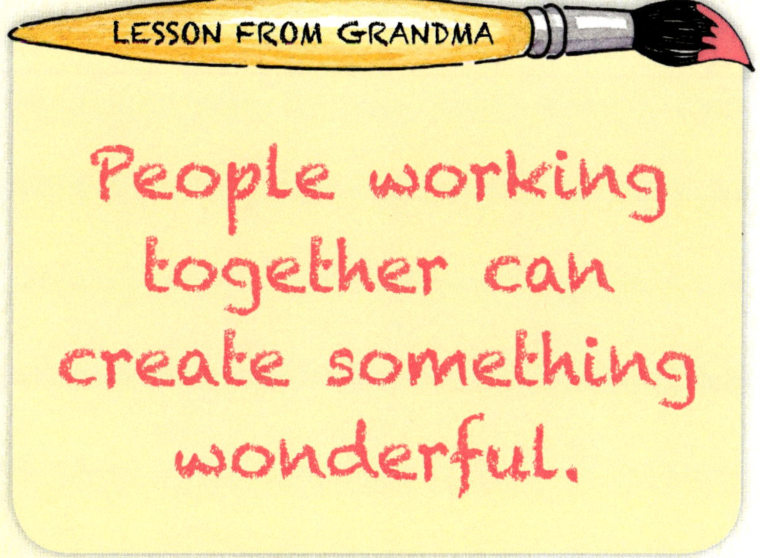

One day, it started raining just when Grandma and I were getting ready to have a picnic at the beach. I was very disappointed and upset. Grandma said not to worry, because we could have a beach picnic inside her house. I didn't think it would work, but she said she had a plan.

First, Grandma found a recipe on the computer for play dough that we could use to make pretend food. It was fun using the play dough to make spaghetti, hot dogs, hamburgers and strawberries. I did such a good job, it looked good enough to eat!

Grandma put a blue rug on the floor to be our ocean. We put on sun hats and turned the lights on really bright so it felt like a sunny day. If I closed my eyes, I could smell the ocean and hear the seagulls.

Another time, I really wanted to go camping in a tent, but I didn't have a tent and Mom never wants to sleep outside with the bugs and animals. I used a big box from a speaker Dad bought to make myself a tent house so I could camp right in my toy room.

I cut a door in the front so I could crawl in and added a window so I could look out. I drew a fireplace on one inside wall and a garden on the opposite inside wall. I put my sleeping bag on the floor inside the box and drew a headboard above it. Then, I decorated the outside, made a roof from strips of foam and created a doorbell from pipe cleaners. I loved going in there and pretending I was outdoors, camping in a beautiful place. Best of all, there were no bugs or animals!

LESSON FROM GRANDMA

I can use my imagination to be anywhere I choose.

At Grandma and Grandpa's house, I don't have video games or toys with batteries. When I go there, I use my imagination to have fun. Their toy closet has all kinds of neat stuff in it. There are hand puppets, puzzles, books, big pads with pictures to color and a treasure chest with dress-up clothes.

From the treasure chest, I can become a pirate, a rock star, a hula girl, Cinderella, or a fairy princess. Grandma laughs when I put on a fashion show for her. She really loves it when I add music and dancing to the show and she usually sings along with me.

LESSON FROM GRANDMA

I don't need electronic toys to have fun.

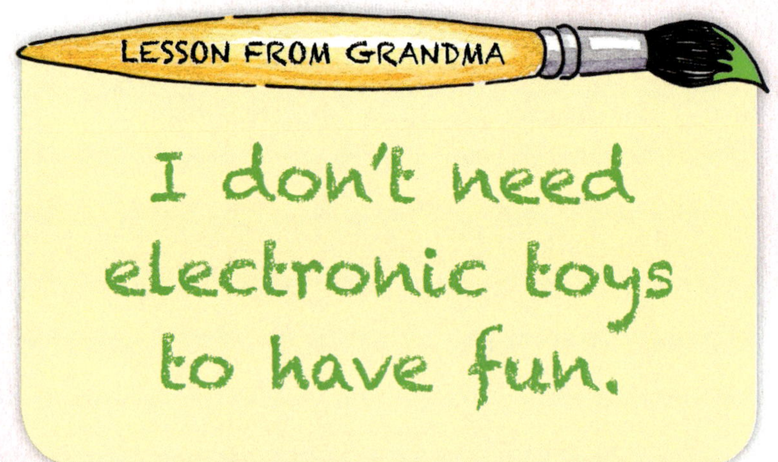

When I was 2, Grandma gave me a big bag of building blocks for my birthday and I keep them at her house. When I was little, every time I played with them, I made the same thing: a big tower that fell over because I built it too high. Now I've learned that if I make a solid base first, I can build bridges, moats and many towers that won't fall over. When my sister or cousins play blocks with me, they keep knocking down the towers! Someday, I'll teach them how to make a base too, so their towers won't fall down.

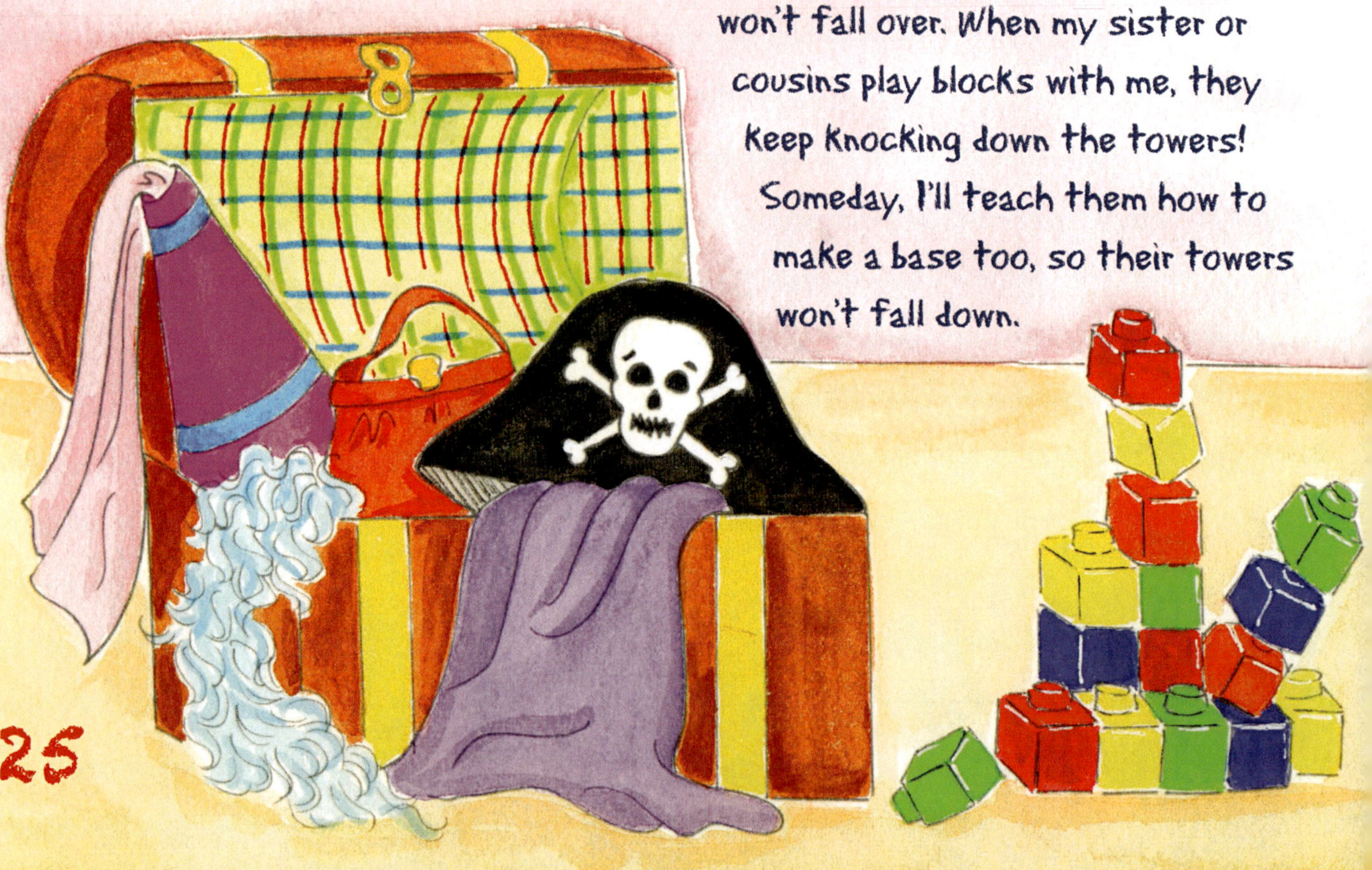

As I got bigger, Grandma let me use her best brushes and her special watercolor paints all the time. She showed me the right way to wet the paints and clean the brush when I changed colors. She showed me how to mix the colors on the big palette and how to use the brushes in different ways.

A couple of years ago, Santa surprised me with a big, canvas bag filled with paints, brushes and paper just for me. Santa must have known I would love this gift, because the bag had my name on it. And it had a real artist palette to hold and mix my paints, just like Grandma's. I sure felt special. This gift felt like a wonderful reward for doing art all the time.

Grandma always tells me that I'm a very important person and there is no one else like me in the whole world. That doesn't mean I can be selfish. It means I have to love myself first and truly believe in myself.

LESSON FROM GRANDMA

I deserve the best.

I love Christmas and I love getting presents from Santa and my family. I also love surprising everyone with gifts I make. Grandma and I have made many wonderful things since I was a little girl. The first gifts we made were from shells Grandma collected on her vacation. She made sure each one had a hole in it so we could put ribbons through the holes to hang them on the Christmas tree. I used many bright colors of glitter glue to decorate the shells and Grandma added the ribbons. My family loved them and now they look forward to seeing what surprises I've made for them every Christmas.

Before I was born, Grandma started a tradition of creating a Christmas card to send to all her friends. Each year, she puts a snowman in a painting she made when she was on vacation. Everyone looks forward to seeing where the snowman will be each Christmas. One time he was in Italy on a boat, one time he was in France in a wine vineyard and many times he was on a beautiful beach.

One year, when Grandma was showing me all the cards she had made, I got the idea of painting one for her. While she was busy working on the computer, I painted a snowman sitting on the cruise ship we took to celebrate my Nana's 80th birthday. When Grandma looked up, I was all finished. She loved my card and decided to send it to all her friends instead of her own snowman. In her message, she told them that I painted it. I was very proud.

My art can be shared with others in many ways.

HAND PAINTED
BOOKMARKS
by MIKAYLA
$1.00

LESSON FROM GRANDMA

I can help others with my art.

Every year, there is a big fair to raise money to help people in our community. Grandma and Mom always work hard at the fair to make it a success. I always have fun there, playing games, getting my face painted and eating lots of goodies.

When I was 6, Grandma and I talked about how I could help raise money at the fair with my art. I decided to make bookmarks and paint them with watercolors. I painted each of the 30 bookmarks with unique designs and colors. Grandpa took them to a store to have plastic put on them. Then, we punched a hole and put bright ribbons in each one. Grandma hung them on clothes hangers to make it easy for everyone to see all the designs and choose which one to buy. They looked great.

I sold them at the fair for $1 each. Everyone loved them and I felt very proud that I was able to contribute $30 to people who needed help. Grandma and Grandpa each bought one and they use them all the time in the books they read.

This year, I'm going to try to get other kids to make lots of bookmarks so we can help many more people.

Grandma says it's important to eat healthy foods so that your brain can work really well. When we're doing art, we eat hummus with vegetables, apples with peanut butter, raisins, yogurt or string cheese. Both my body and my brain feel better when I have these foods.

Even though you get hungry when you're being creative, never eat the crayons or paints. They'll make you very sick!

Art helps keep my mind healthy too. If I feel sad or scared, I can share my feelings by putting them on paper. Art always makes me feel better.

LESSON FROM GRANDMA

Art is healthy.

One summer, Grandma took a picture of me blowing bubbles at her pool. I think she took it just to remember the great time we had that day. But it became much more important. Grandma sent the picture to a newspaper to use for an article about happy summer memories. It felt really weird seeing my face in the newspaper and knowing that many other people would see it.

She used that same picture to make a pastel painting of me on a day when she was very upset. She told me that putting all the love she felt for me on the paper made her smile and feel so much better. The painting is so great it won an award in an art show.

Grandma used another photo she had taken to paint a portrait of me at the beach with Grandpa. She gave it to Grandpa as a Christmas gift and he loved it. I love it too. In the painting, Grandpa is holding my hand and you can see he is taking good care of me. When I look at it, I feel loved and safe. Grandma was able to put that feeling in her painting. It's difficult to do, but she's teaching me how.

I like to use my imagination in many ways. When Grandma took me to a museum with an exhibit about the environment, I spent most of my time in the Green Art Room. It was filled with things people donated to the museum instead of throwing them away. The room had lots of plastic bottles, fabrics, bottle caps, buttons, markers, glue, Styrofoam, pipe cleaners, cotton balls and glitter. The room was part of the exhibit, showing us how to be creative with things that usually go in the garbage. I had a great time making a bride doll from a plastic bottle and fabric.

After that day at the museum, Grandma started saving all kinds of weird things and we found many new ways to use them.

One day, Grandma and I created a room for my doll from a cardboard box turned on its side and plastic containers from her organic vegetables and fruits. I made a rug out of construction paper and cut a picture out of the comics to be a flat-screen TV. A matchbook covered with paper became the TV remote. We made a canopy for the plastic bed from straws and some old doilies and used a paper cup to make a lamp. I really enjoyed playing with it before my sister tore it apart.

LESSON FROM GRANDMA

We can help the environment and have fun with things other people don't need anymore.

MATH
PLANNING
LANGUAGE
Oui Si YES!
SCIENCE
ART
IMAGINATION
MUSIC
IDEAS
PLAYING
DREAMING
FIGHTING
YELLING

LESSON FROM GRANDMA

Art can help me succeed in school.

Grandma told me there are two parts of your brain that need to work together as you learn. The left side of the brain plans and remembers things. That's the logical side. The right side is the creative side. That's where art happens and where you can find solutions to problems. When both sides work together, it's like magic.

Last year, my teacher told us to do a report for a book we really liked. She didn't want us to just write sentences about it. She wanted us to do something creative. I talked this over with Grandma and I decided I could make a poster for my report. The book was *David Goes to School* by David Shannon. It was the story about a boy who made many bad choices in school. He was always getting in trouble and people were always saying, "No, David."

Working with both sides of my brain, I created a poster with a drawing of David in the middle and pictures of all the bad choices he had made around the outside. It looked really cool. The poster made it easy for me to talk about the book in school and my teacher gave me a smiley face for my report.

LESSON FROM GRANDMA

Watch sunsets! Each one is unique, just like every person.

There are many things I love about being at Grandma's house, especially the beach and the birds. I've learned about shells and birds from her books. Together, we notice the special colors and shapes of each one. Making art has taught me to really look at everything carefully.

In the winter, the sun sets right in front of Grandma's patio. Since I was a little girl, we've always watched the colors in the sky and the meadows change as the sun goes down. The scene looks different each time and I love to watch the colors surprise me. Grandma has always helped me appreciate how special these differences are and now I really understand.

One day, when the sun started to go down, I told Grandma that I wanted to paint it and remember it always. I knew I wouldn't see that same sky any other day. Grandma gave me her paints and said I would have to work fast since the sun disappears very quickly.

I loved looking at this beautiful scene and painting the colors I saw. I was so excited; I was practically bouncing out of my seat. Mom framed the painting right away and hung it in our living room. When I walk past it, I remember that special moment.

You might be surprised to know that you can make art in the bathtub. But Grandma bought special painting bubble bath for me so I could make abstract art in her big bathtub.

You might not think that you can make art while you're waiting for breakfast. But I do. Grandma bought a big sketchbook for me to take when I go out to breakfast with Grandpa. One day, I made a drawing of the grill with eggs, bacon and pancakes. The owner of the restaurant loved it. He asked if he could buy it and paid me with a brownie. Then he hung my drawing in a place where everyone could see it. I loved seeing it there.

You can even make art in the library. Before I started school, Grandpa took me to library story time every Thursday. The librarian read us a story and then we made a craft about it. That's where I really got to practice my cutting and gluing. Now, Grandpa takes my sister, Maya. Because I'm in school, I can only go to story time and crafts in the summer. Even though I'm in 3rd grade now, I still love going to the library to make art.

LESSON FROM GRANDMA

Art can happen anywhere.

I also made art when I was in Disney World. I used my notebook to write about my trip and make drawings of gifts Mickey Mouse left in our room. One night after I was finished with dessert, I drew a portrait of Maya eating her ice cream. She loved posing for it and I think it made her feel special. When I look at the picture, I remember all the wonderful things about my trip!

LESSON FROM GRANDMA

Stories can be told with art in many ways.

Grandma told me about a famous African American artist, Faith Ringgold, who tells stories with her art in many ways. Sometimes she tells a story in a painting. Sometimes she tells a story in a book or a song. Other times, she makes quilts and each square has words and pictures on it to tell a story. One day Grandma is going to take me to see Faith Ringgold's beautiful quilts in a museum.

When I was little, I loved to staple paper together and make art books with lots of drawings and paintings. Now I can add words to my pages so the books tell a story. Sometimes, it's a story about fun things we've done or a special day we've had. Sometimes it's a story about my family and how much I love them. Grandma calls this kind of book a journal.

I've learned that I can express my feelings in these books and everyone likes to read them. I think it will be great to save them and read them when I get older. Grandma has a whole box of her own journals that she has filled with drawings and words about her feelings. That's how she got the idea for this book.

Grandma and I work with lots of art materials. We can create art in many ways and it's exciting to see how each material works. I love to go in the closet where she keeps all her art materials: pastel crayons, fabric paints, acrylic paints, pipe cleaners, glitter glue, stickers and all kinds of paper.

Most of the materials are pretty easy to use and aren't very messy, but the pottery wheel Aunt Mandy gave me for my birthday was a challenge. The directions told us to make the clay soft by squeezing it between our fingers and putting water on it. Next, the directions said to put the clay on the wheel, start the wheel spinning and put our fingers inside to make a vase or a bowl.

It was a lot harder and messier than we expected. We had clay up to our elbows. Dust flew all over Grandma's art studio. We laughed and had a great time even though one vase came out lopsided, the handle on the bowl broke and the shell I was making for Aunt Linnie collapsed.

Grandma explained that when we try something new, things may not come out the way we plan. She taught me to accept feeling frustrated because it means I'm really learning. I have to work on that because it still feels uncomfortable.

LESSON FROM GRANDMA
Always look for
the beauty in
people, places
and the world
around me.

I have learned the names of all the beautiful colors Grandma uses in her paintings. One of her favorite colors is cerulean blue, the color of the ocean and the sky on a really sunny day. Grandma sees beauty everywhere and her paintings make people feel happy.

I love going to Grandma's art shows. I sit with her and watch people smile when they see her paintings of beaches, castles and all the places she has visited. I'm so glad people like her paintings and buy them to keep always.

Grandma has taught me that some artists express themselves with pictures that have different colors or subjects than hers. Some of these pictures may feel sad or sometimes even scary. But Grandma has shown me this is another form of beauty.

The important thing is to really look at what is around you in the world. Grandma has taught me to notice the shapes of clouds, the delicate colors of flowers and the unique patterns on butterfly wings. She says that there is beauty in diversity. Beauty can even be found in the big, dark night sky or in the contrast of the yellow-and-black stripes on a tiny bumblebee.

Before I was born, Grandma stopped working at a big company and started spending time with artists. Now she has a company that gives art classes in a wonderful place by the ocean. She told me that being with artists gives her lots of energy. It helps her to be creative and have good ideas. This year, she also started a painting group where she lives and has made lots of new friends. She says it's much better than taking the train to work every day!

At the beginning of 3rd grade, I had an idea for making an art club with my friends at school. Every day, we'd each draw or paint a card during recess and then trade them with each other. When I told Grandma about my idea, she was very excited. She helped me cut cards from her big watercolor paper. Then I made packages for each of my friends with their names on them. Grandma says when we have a lot of cards, it would be interesting to put them together and make a big collage.

I love being an artist and spending time with Grandma using my creativity and imagination. It's comfortable and fun making art together. As I get older, I want to have a lot of artist friends. I'll spend time with them the way Grandma does, even if I have to take the train to work.

Grandma has so much love in her heart that she can give lots of love and attention to all her grandchildren. I was the first grandchild, so I was lucky to have her all to myself for 4 years. My first cousin, Kylie, was born when I was 4 and my little sister, Maya, was born when I was 5. Then, two more cousins, Jordan and Noah, were born when I was 6 and 8.

My cousins live far away and Grandma doesn't see them very often. But when she does, she teaches them to use their creativity too. I have an idea to start an art club with my cousins. Now that I have my own e-mail address, I think we can send our art to each other through the Internet and make books for Grandma. And when my cousins visit, we can do art and other creative things with Grandma. We can collaborate and make wonderful memories.

I was a little worried that Grandma would love me less when all the other kids in my family came along. Now, I see that she can love all of her grandchildren at the same time. And we love her right back with all our hugs and kisses! She says that you can never run out of hugs and kisses.

LESSON FROM GRANDMA

The more love you give, the more you get back.

When I was a little girl, my world felt loving and kind. Now that I'm 8, I realize the world can be a really tough place sometimes. There are bullies at school. There are wars and angry people who don't get along with others. There are people who don't have enough food or people to love them.

Grandma has learned that art can help make the world a better place. She showed me that if people try to find beauty instead of ugliness, they will see beauty. If they're making art or appreciating art, they won't be mean to others. If they're sad or angry, they can express these feelings with art instead of hurting others.

I just learned about two world leaders who were artists: Winston Churchill and Dwight D. Eisenhower. Mr. Eisenhower was American. He was a general in the army and became president of the United States when Grandma was a little girl. Winston Churchill was a British prime minister. Even though these men lived in different parts of the world, they were friends and they worked together to bring peace to Europe during a big war. They both made beautiful oil paintings of places they visited and people they knew. While they were in charge of their countries, they always made time to paint. Both Prime Minister Churchill and President Eisenhower believed that doing art helped them make better decisions for their countries and the world.

I know I want to use my art in a way that helps others and shows them beauty so they will feel good. This is the most important art lesson I have learned.

MIKAYLA'S EPILOGUE

I am now almost 10 years old and in the 4th grade. I am having lots of new experiences and trying many new things. I go to a new school where I change classrooms, make new friends and have a locker for the first time. Decorating our lockers was a really big deal. Mine has peace signs on the walls, pictures of my family, a curtain and even a chandelier. Each of my friends' lockers has its own style.

At school, I have joined several clubs during recess for art, music, gymnastics and reading. Each of the members is unique and I think that will make the clubs interesting. When Grandma heard what I was doing, she said it was amazing.

While Grandma was working on our book, she was also creating an art show at our church. It was awesome. Grandma had the kids in the church's school make little paintings that she called "mini treasures," so Maya and I got to be in the same show as Grandma. A newspaper wrote an article about this happening. How cool is that?

Grandma and I now do art with my sister, Maya. She is different from me and it's hard to teach her to be patient. She stops, stomps and leaves the room with an attitude when she's heard enough. I was more patient; that's why Grandma has been able to teach me so many important lessons. But, while I sometimes have trouble thinking about what to paint, Maya just does it from the top of her head. She's very courageous and has a great sense of style. So, I think she will be a great artist too and learn all of Grandma's lessons in her own way. Maybe she will be what Grandma calls an action painter, like Jackson Pollock, who dribbled paint on huge canvases in colorful patterns. Maybe she will be a fashion designer or a dancer.

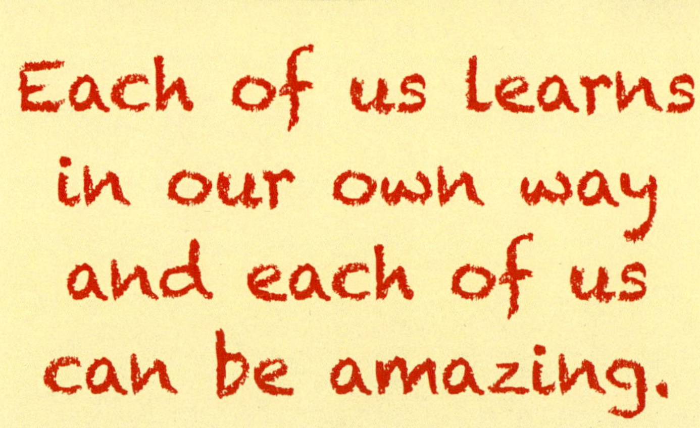

MY NAME IS

MY DRAWING IS CALLED

Grandma, Maya and me

Maya, the action painter

Maya's first painting

Maya, the funny French artist

Maya, the dancing queen

Fun on the haystacks

A great day at the Crayola Crayon Factory

The bags we created on vacation

HOW THIS BOOK WAS CREATED

I am the Grandma in *Art Lessons from Grandma.*

After hearing my many stories about the wonderful times I've had making art with my granddaughter Mikayla, a friend suggested I write a book. I started thinking about this.

I asked Mikayla what she thought and I realized that my passion for art had been passed along to her as we painted and played together.

Mikayla at age 2 with Grandma

The first step was doing video interviews to discover Mikayla's memories. It was thrilling for me to find out that she gets it. She talked about the importance of art in my life and how she was grateful that I was sharing my delight with her. She told lots of stories about how she learned about me and about life while we made art together. Her enthusiasm told me that art is as important to her as it is to me.

For the past fifteen years, I've wanted to share the magic of how art positively impacts life. I've always had a positive attitude, been a cheerleader to those around me and introduced friends and clients to the magic of seeing the world through an artist's eyes. I've inspired and encouraged them to move past their comfort zones to see the many possibilities that stretch out before them. Telling our story through Mikayla's words has given me the chance to share my passion with a wider audience and to be a cheerleader to many more people.

Art Lessons from Grandma illustrates how doing art and using one's imagination teaches important life lessons, bolsters self-esteem and builds loving relationships. I wanted this book to appeal to both children and adults, because I strongly believe that making art is one of the best ways to feed one's soul and make the world a better place.

Denise Weiner

MIKAYLA'S DEFINITIONS OF IMPORTANT WORDS

Abstraction: a fantasy picture.
Appreciate: to enjoy or like something even if you don't understand it.
Collaboration: being creative and working together as a team on an idea or a painting.
Collage: a picture made with different objects that you find, such as paper, glue, feathers or glitter.
Cooperation: including others, listening to what they say and working together as a team.
Creativity: having an idea about something you never knew before and doing something on your own that's really, really good.
Diversity: different cultures, people, food, styles and clothes.
Express: to draw a picture to show how you feel.
Hummus: really good food made with beans that you can dip carrots and pretzels in.
Inspiring: cheering, helping and encouraging another person.
Journal: a book where you can brainstorm or sketch. You can share it with others, or it can be a diary where you keep your secret stuff.
Mixed-media: artwork made with different materials: watercolor, pencils, markers, ink or crayons.
Perspective: the way you think about a problem or look at a painting.
Palette: a tray to hold your paints and mix your colors.
Tradition: something special you do with your family every day or every year at holidays.
Unique: special, different, or really awesome.

BIOGRAPHIES OF IMPORTANT PEOPLE IN THE BOOK

Artists

Georgia O'Keeffe: 1887–1986. She was an American artist who was one of the most important modern painters in America. Her large flowers and Southwestern landscapes are very famous.

Pablo Picasso: 1881–1973. He was a Spanish artist who began formal art training when he was 7 years old. During his life, he went through many different periods of creativity, including the Blue Period, the Rose Period and Cubism.

Jackson Pollock: 1912–1956. He was an American painter well known for his drip-style painting on very large canvases and his abstract expressionism.

Faith Ringgold: 1930– . She is an African American artist who tells stories with her art. Her quilts with words and pictures are very beautiful.

Cy Twombly: 1928–2011. He was an American artist, well known for large, freely scribbled, graffiti-type paintings.

Andy Warhol: 1928–1987. He was an American artist who was the leader of pop art. Among his most famous works are Campbell's soup cans and colorful portraits of famous people.

Authors

David Shannon, *David Goes to School*

Crockett Johnson, *Harold and the Purple Crayon*

Wally Piper, *The Little Engine That Could*

Famous People

Dwight D. Eisenhower: 1890–1969. He was a five-star general in the army, leading the US forces during World War II. He was the president of Columbia University and the 34th president of the United States. He started painting when he was 40 years old as a way to relax and he had an art studio in the White House.

Winston Churchill: 1874–1965. He was a British prime minister and he played an important role in bringing peace to Europe following World War II. He wrote many volumes on British history and war and won a Nobel Prize for literature. He discovered painting when he was 49 years old and painted many landscapes and portraits during his lifetime.

FUN THINGS YOU CAN MAKE TOGETHER

Play Dough

Mix together 2 cups flour, 1 cup salt and 1 cup water with food coloring. If the mixture is too sticky, add a little flour until it feels right. Making funny faces while you're mixing makes the dough even better. Put the dough in a baggie so it doesn't dry out.

Squeeze-Bottle Glitter

Mix equal parts of flour, salt, and water. Pour into plastic squeeze bottles, like the ones mustard and ketchup come in. Add food coloring to each bottle while you sing your favorite song. Squeeze the glitter onto heavy construction paper or cardboard. When your designs are dry, the salt makes them sparkle just like the stars at night.

Colored Pasta

In a small baggie, add 2 handfuls of uncooked pasta and food coloring. Seal the baggie and shake until the pasta is colored. Play lively music and dance around during the baggie shaking part. Lay the pasta on paper towels to dry.

Baked Clay

Mix together 1 cup flour, 1/2 cup salt and 1/2 cup warm water. Knead (squeeze and squish the clay between your fingers), create your shapes and bake at 200 degrees for 2 hours. Then paint your masterpieces with acrylic paint.

Giant Chocolate Sculpted Cookies To Eat

Ingredients

2 sticks of butter
1 1/2 cups sugar
3 eggs
1 tablespoon vanilla
3 3/4 cups flour
3/4 cup cocoa powder
1/4 teaspoon salt
3/4 teaspoon baking soda
Mini M&M's or chocolate chips for decoration

Yield: 12 large cookies

Directions

1. Preheat oven to 350 degrees.
2. Combine butter and sugar until light and fluffy. Add eggs and vanilla.
3. Combine the dry ingredients—flour, cocoa, baking soda and salt. Sift together.
4. Add the dry ingredients to the butter and sugar mixture. Gather together and flatten into a disk. Chill until firm, about 1 hour.
5. Divide dough into 12 equal pieces. Form into desired shape or character, such as Minnie Mouse, approximately 1/2 inch thick.
6. Decorate with mini M&M's or chocolate chips.
7. Bake on parchment-lined pans for 10 to 12 minutes. Remove to racks to cool. Do not over bake.

Giant Chocolate Sculpted Cookie recipe Courtesy of Cook 'N' Tell, a cooking school in Colts Neck, New Jersey, for adults and children. Visit their website at www.cookntell.com.

FUN RESOURCES FOR CREATIVE EXPRESSION

Things you have in your home

- Cardboard boxes, egg crates and cardboard tubes
- Plastic bottles and bubble wrap
- String, straws, ribbons, fabric and buttons
- Paper, glue, stapler and paper clips

Things you can buy inexpensively

- Nontoxic art supplies from Clementine Art (www.clementineart.com)
- Professional, high quality art materials from Cheap Joes (www.cheapjoes.com)
- Materials from office supply stores when they're on sale

Places you can go

- Your public library has tons of free resources: story time, arts and crafts, movies, shows.
- Community centers and local museums also offer many free resources.
- County and community parks, theatres, museums are great places to go.
- Your friend's home—start your own playgroup.

Internet resources

Make sure an adult gives you permission to use the Internet to access any of these sites:

www.family.go.com—visit this site sponsored by Disney to get ideas for crafts and recipes, printable coloring pages, party ideas and holiday ideas. You can also register for their free newsletter.

www.hulafrog.com—this is a terrific site where you can learn about what's going on near your home. Register to be notified about local family activities—many of which are free.

www.kids.yahoo.com—there is a wealth of great stuff on this site including games, music, video clips, e-cards and a fun search engine for kids.

www.fisher-price.com —you will find crafts and activities to do together, ideas for outings and online games. You can also request their free newsletter, "Grandest Times."

HOW TO SHARE YOUR CREATIVE EXPERIENCES AND LIFE LESSONS WITH US

Mikayla and I know that you will love this book and that its lessons can be life changing at any age. We want to hear about the lessons you have learned as you use creative activities to build a loving relationship with your child or grandchild. We would also love to see the art you make together and learn about ideas you have for other creative activities and resources.

- You can email us at artlessonsfromgrandma@comcast.net
- You can add your comments and artwork to our website: www.artlessonsfromgrandma.com

BIBLIOGRAPHY

Churchill, Minnie, and David Coombs. *Sir Winston Churchill: His Life and His Paintings.* Philadelphia: Running Press, 2004.

Eisenhower, Dwight D. *Pictures I've Kept.* Garden City: Doubleday and Company, 1969.

Eisenhower, Dwight D. *At Ease: Stories I Tell to Friends.* Garden City: Doubleday and Company, 1967.

INDEX OF ART FORMS

This index will help you find examples of different art forms in the book.

DENISE WEINER

Denise's journey from corporate America to an art studio began fifteen years ago with a watercolor class at a spa. That experience led her on a journey of formal painting classes, art trips to Europe and ultimately the decision to end her successful career in the corporate sector. Denise is now living her dream life filled with art, travel, writing and enjoying her five grandchildren. With over thirty years in communications, marketing and international business, she has learned that art and play enhance everyone's professional and personal life.

Denise has passed along her passion for art and creativity to her grandchildren. She has been able to spend the last ten years painting and teaching her grandchildren about life as they paint together. *Art Lessons from Grandma* is her first published book.

Denise lives in Port Monmouth, New Jersey, with her husband, Mark.

MIKAYLA HOUSTON

Mikayla is in the fourth grade and lives in Holmdel, New Jersey, with her mom, dad, and sister, Maya. She loves art, music, writing, singing, dancing and anything creative.

MARIE T. MARTINELLI

Marie is a talented artist, working primarily in watercolor and pastel. She also runs a successful business designing and sewing special occasion dresses for little girls and making custom dolls. She has two daughters and two young grandchildren who are the joys of her life.

Denise and Marie have been friends for many years and working on this book together has been a wonderful experience.

Marie lives in Middletown, New Jersey with her husband, Lou.

MY NAME IS

MY DRAWING IS CALLED

MY NAME IS

MY DRAWING IS CALLED

MY NAME IS

MY DRAWING IS CALLED